*From a fellow human who has too many feelings
and lives in constant disgust of them.*

Acknowledgements

A sincere thanks to my remarkably fragile heart for getting so affected by mild inconveniences that I had to write about them.

Also, to friends & family for being sweethearts, mostly.

Table Of Contents

Ideal Poetry

Poetry should be
about metaphors, similes,
allegories and hidden connotations.
Words intertwined so delicately
that your fingertips scorch when you
untangle them to decipher.
Poetry should be so complex that
you pull your hair, forget eating
your breakfast, check dim lit
libraries for reference books.
Poetry should be arresting
and enchanting, it should be
a melancholy or yearning.
Give me flowers here,
fancy words, take me
through the extravagant
palace of your vocabulary.

Come on, throw ornate
language at mama!

Or not.
Show me patternless
drawings of your words,
the unembellished, raw ones.
The ones that you hide in
your 'edit later' folder only because
it isn't ornamented enough.

I'd ask poetry to just be
for the way you talk about
how you're tired of always wanting
to pee in winters make me beam like
a moron. It's poetic. You are poetic.
You're sometimes not flowery,
you are gunshots and filth
but I wouldn't have it any other way.
In all your plain words and simplicity,
you are still a poem to me.

An Insincere Love Letter To My City

I don't do very well with my city,
I like to think of it longingly
and talk about it only reverently
but if truth be told we don't
really get along.

It's like a lover who you know
a little too much about to
want to move in with and
you earnestly don't want to
pick fights over plastic
straws, littered streets and this
weird obsession of sun with you
glaring at your face all day non-stop.
You know it's got a pink sky,
matching buildings and is beautiful
but you also know better so you like
to steer clear of its compelling
but vacant blue eyes.

You like leaving it,
abruptly and often.

A little scared every time
that it may not want
you back someday.
Afterall, it knows you too;
about your empty promises;
insincere love letters and of you
philandering with other cities.

My Body Is Mad At You

I wish the blades on my back
could cut you in two or thirteen
as you sneer at my body.
And, my legs could entangle
like two snakes in love and
swallow you whole to
compensate for the extra meat
that you think I so badly need.

I wish my curves or their lack thereof
bother you so much that they remind
you of all that you will never have.

And for once,
for once,

my mouth would not
remain shut as you feel free to
pronounce your valued observations.
I wish it would remain as witty and
as lethal so that I don't have
to work extra hard to plan
your funeral.

Don't Make Me Look

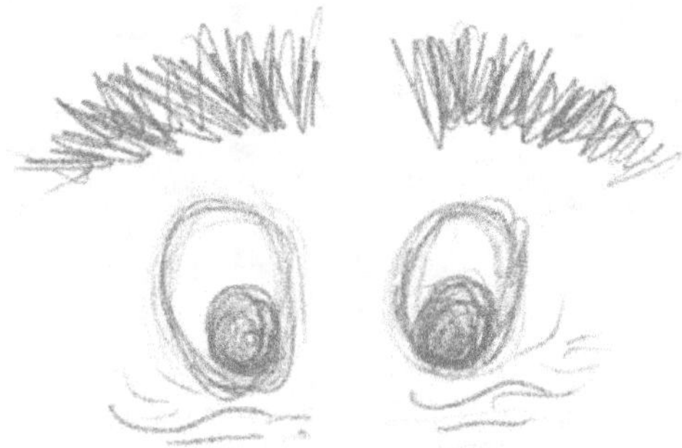

Looking around saddens me.

To fix what is broken,
I take the most obvious route.

I look around lesser.

Instead, I try looking at my
palms to remind myself that there
is only so much that they can offer.

And that, I shall not try to amend
what does not belong to me.

I look around lesser now to
find out who it all belongs to.

But after every two fortnights,
like a sacred ritual, my pen
and I bleed pathetically.

I whine and rant and
go on and on.

I lay my heart bare
on paper for you to read.

But then I understand,
you too are trying to look
around less.

Aren't you?

Announcement

On the days when you are too tired
to make sense of the world,
or the world can't make
sense of your words.

When weight from bags that don't
belong to you start going to the luggage
storage room in your head.

The days being mentioned are
when the charm around listening,
understanding, being there on your toes
with a proud cape flowing with the air,
loses its shine and gets a little

dull and dimmer.

Baby, that's when you dim the lights too.

Or maybe, turn them off.

Listen to the quiet.

If that doesn't work,
listen to fix you from Coldplay
and wait for the magic.

Your powers shall be restored
within 3-5 business days.
Please rest assured that they will
be returned to you at the earliest,
because there is so much yet
to be listened to.
So much weight still waiting
to be lifted.

Thank you for listening!

I Talked To A Bird

I swear I talked to a bird today.
See, I hate when you make that
face in disbelief all the time.

The bird looked at me funny too.

Then, I saw it descend gracefully
towards my nose. I wonder if that's
the only thing about me visible from afar.

It asked me not to touch
the flower I was playing with.

And then, I looked at it funny.
But its beak looked a little
too sharp for me to have beef
with it so I just asked, "Why?"

The stupid bird told me,
"Look bruh, I love this flower
ardently. The dew on its pink has
bewitched me – body and soul.
I fly down every morning from
wherever I am to make sure nobody
else gets to witness it before me.
Long story short, this flower belongs
to me and I will not see you
around it again."

I didn't realize how absurd
that was until the bird said it.
It used to make perfect sense
to me when people put their
love like that.

But, I put my hands in my
pocket and walked away.
I didn't want no beef.

Too Much Feeling Happening

Some days I feel so much that
my body is unable to contain my heart
so I spill it on the last pages of the notebook,
paint it on my denims and make clumsy
paper boats out of my feelings
and proudly call them origami.

I might not listen to you when
you tell me that my paper boats suck
because on these days, I am unreasonably
headstrong and proud and you'd be
talking over the voices in my head
which by then must already be plotting
to make you sail in my paper boats
to somewhere far away.

Climb a tree with me on such days,
or watch the sky pour from distance
while it howls or chuckles.

Or watch me as I devour ice cream
but please sit quietly and know that
we are friends despite me
not wanting to talk.

Because on these days
I am quiet, even more
than the usual.

I thought it's important
to let you know this while
I am not.

Oh also,
on these days or otherwise
please don't ask for a
share of my ice-cream.

On Loving And Living

When I was 8, and thought I would grow up
to be somebody great, my father had
once sat me down.

He then sat across me as I looked at him curiously,
took my hand, and asked me to make a promise.
He seemed so earnest I reached out to my lap
and unconsciously closed the comics.

I assumed this to be a matter of grave concern
but to my surprise, the conversation had
already taken a sharp turn.

He started off by telling stories from his
childhood with no beginnings or ends.
They were sure absurdly funny
but I couldn't see how they would help me
in crucial matters, like making money.

There was so much to do.
My favorite characters used to keep

calling me at night to ask if I had
any special gifts too.

To give him a hint that he must
not waste any of my precious time,
I looked at my watch.
After all, I had to go and be top notch.

He then laughed at me and said,
"Promise me dove, that you will never
be so obsessed about making it big that you
forget about the stories that you are so fond of.
I want you to make time for things that matter,
always, over and above, lay your head back as
you laugh, offer the world whatever little you can
but most importantly, I want you to make
a living by doing what you love."

I Live In A Far-Off Place

I live in a far-off place, miles away from here.

To reach, you shall have to take a right and
then left from the 'Lane of No Care.'
You might want to take off those fancy shoes
and put on your everyday slippers,
for the land where I live hosts no parties,
balls or dinners.

The rustling of leaves and the chirrups
might be a little deafening for you.
However, you will love all of it if you
too are dressed in blue.

The closer to my home you come,
the quieter it might get.
The trees shall give you directions
only in sign language, they haven't
learnt the low-born tongue of words yet.

If you are lucky,

my horse will ferry you around
from there without the slightest fuss.

And if not, you shall keep walking for days
without finding food, phone's network or a bus.

When you reach, please ring the doorbell.
I obviously understand that shall be after you have
seen the frozen chocolate castle and are not
anymore under its spell.

This would be one way to reach me,
the other would be to wake me up and
remind it's just all in my head.
But I'd rather you come and meet
me there or having unimaginative
friends is honestly the only thing I dread.

Pigeons Rule

In a parallel universe
or an alternate reality,
pigeons win.

They rule.

They read
and they write
better than
Plath and Whitman.

You, on the other hand,
helplessly carry their letters
tied tightly on your leg
to their pigeon friends,
relatives and associates
without objections.

Stop Your Idle Dreaming

Yes, sit down please.
No! Not beside me halfwit.
Across me, yes there.

How else will I look into the empty parts of you?

You have been painting, I see.
What's the point in hiding when I already know?
Show me your hands. No, not like that.
The palms. Keep them on the table.
Here, yes.

Did your painting not have a sky or what?
Why isn't there any shade of blue on your hands?

What do you mean the sky was pink?
See, this is why I don't like you watching movies.

You should by now know
what is what, what gives what
and what does what.

What you should also know is

'What' is an interrogative pronoun.

Who got you colors? Which drawer?
No, they are not mine. They can't be.
I hid mine years ago.
They didn't get me anywhere.
You shouldn't look for things where
you are not supposed to, understand?
And, don't ask questions.

Now, listen carefully.
We will go back home, throw them
away and never speak of it again.
What do you mean I got colors in my eyes?
Stop dreaming so foolishly.

Writing As A Friend

Tonight, I shall write to you as a friend.

I shall write as the weird geeky guy
in your classroom who you thought
was creepy initially because he observed
so much about you that you wanted to
have nothing to do with him or
anybody of that sort.

Only to realize later, that he knew
what you took years to figure out.
He knew in his heart all about you
that this planet is perhaps blinded to.

The entire planet! Can you imagine?
Well, except your dog who also

somehow knows how you have struggled
with the day, the traffic lights and the
latch of that dumb door before opening
opening your arms to him.

I want to write to you selflessly, like a friend,
without seeking appreciation or gratitude.

I want to write about everything beguiling about you
so that you realize that it does not go unnoticed.

I want to write to you as someone familiar
who you don't remember anymore.

I want to write to you, without corruption and with all
my sincerity so that on the days when you feel
unloved you remember that you have a distant lover too.

I want to write to you so that you know
you'll be okay and for days when you won't be
I am here.

Is It The Chair Spinning Or My Head?

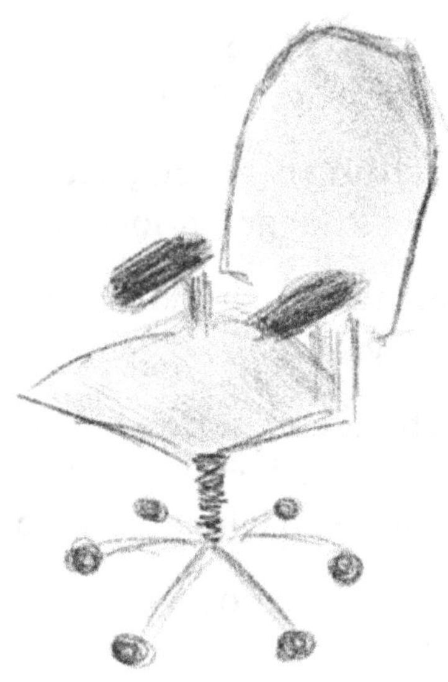

So, I sat back again.
Not on an old rocking chair
like in those creepy movies, by the way,
which creaks and squeaks and yells
and moans every time you fidget.

This one is new, all black,
with wheels to spin,
like she could go to places
if she wanted to but she doesn't
do much, you see.

She is like me.
So, I made friends with the chair,
thinking we will relate well.

She talked about her monochromatic fixation
and I told her all about my overly colorful life.

I asked her, if she knew how to handle one?
She obviously won't know, would she?
We don't relate much now.

We kinda small talk sometimes,
about the city and the weather.
And, when I have more to blabber,
she mostly listens.
She does it well, by the way,
she probably likes me, she should.
I am definitely lighter than anyone
who has sat on her before.

We don't talk much about people, though.
They confuse me.
They are so much like me yet
so much like each other.
I don't need my chair
spinning all the time too.

Blue Days

What do we do on blue days.
We buy ourselves blue flowers
and take long walks on pavements
that are hard as mountain rock
but only think of them as the wet
and green beneath our feet.

We ask for some people's candies
and not talk to the ones we don't want to.

We sing songs that our neighbors find uncool
and brew coffee so dark that even our humor goes,
"the hell, bruh?"

We turn the fairy lights off
and sleep on a white pillow,
we ask the black to be and wake us
up when our hands are again yellow.

We then hop out of bed
on the next grey morning and

ask the black to scooch.

We water ourselves and the plants,
get real mad at it all only to loudly say 'bubbles',
We then quieten and sit in an armchair
to laugh ardently at our own troubles.

Women From Hell

There must be a special place in hell
for women who send postcards along
with pressed flowers that smell less like
flowers and more like them and

ask you to take them to old places
or museums so that they can hear you talk.

Women who make you talk,
and then listen.

The ones who remember your
childhood stories by heart and totally
get your fear of clowns and call out on
your bullshit when you act like one.

The kind of women who finish
your sentences when you're struggling
for the right word, have tasted the
women in your past through your
mouth and only found them as
beautiful as you.

Women who don't mean to
get in your way but end up
growing on you ..
and then leave.

There must be a very
special place in hell for them.

Poems Are Beautiful Because

You know why poems are
so breathtaking?
or heartbreaking?

Because they fucking say it.

Don't ask me they say what.

They say what you can't
or can but don't or
when you do, you suck
at it big big time!

They say it because
that is all they know.

They say that bookstores are erotic,
tenderness is endangered,
men should cry more often,
and your mother is beautiful.

You like them because
you already know all of it.
Poems just say it nicely,
simply, like you should,
dumbfuck.

Just saying it will make you beautiful too.

Dinner Date With My Troubles

Last night I invited my
tiny little troubles over dinner.
They readily came floating like bubbles.
It was an absolute honor to have them over.

They have always been only a call away,
earlier we used to hang out more often though,
sometimes every day.

They devoured all my joy and my happy thoughts,
dug their filthy nails in my flesh and ate
everything on the table and the kitchen.
Trust me, there were lots.

Then they looked at me with wine-stained lips
and gooey eyes as if they had missed me bad.
I had almost forgotten for how long
I had not really been that sad.

I managed to save the last cookie
of hope from yesterday's feast.
I have seen that little thing
grow over the years and
become a beast.

I somehow always happen
to save this tiny bit of cookie.

I'll tell you a secret,
it becomes infinite when
nobody is looking and
saves me.

Damn You, Covid

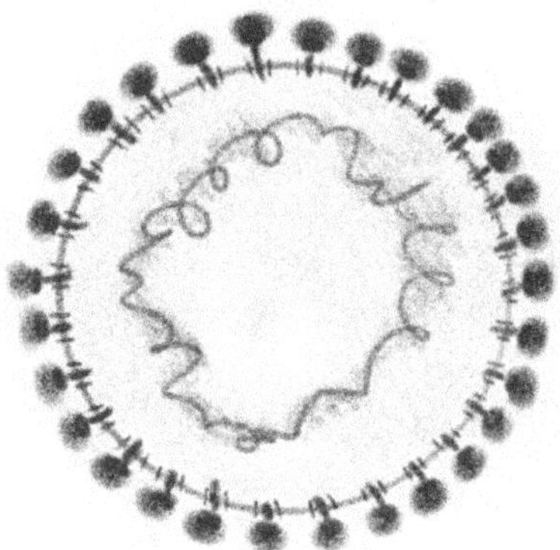

I like being alone.

I love the idea of cancelled plans, staying indoors,
shutting the world out with my earphones plugged in;
listening to some random song on repeat
like Sunflower by Post Malone.

I like the sound of no sound.
I hate to admit this before you but the hours I love
the most are when there is no one around.

I never understand the loud banter
or unrequited small talk,
concepts of socializing, networking …
oh, and for heaven's sake,
adventures like stepping out.

But right now, if you ask me how
I am doing over emails or
a call probably, as we can't meet,
duh .. obviously, I might drop my vanity
and tell you that I am done introverting, truly.

I'm sorry extroverts for all the bashing I ever did.

All the evil things I said in my head when you forced me to hang
out with you, thoughts as vile as acid.

I hope you know now that the
world needs your heart laughter,
casual conversations, picnics
and outings and the days that you
magically turn brighter.

The world needs you.
and I do too.
Please be yourself, as soon
as this ends, boo.

Should I Get A Tattoo?

There is a species of purple flowers that grows in
Balkans which symbolizes honesty.
It's been named Honesty due
to obvious and lethargic reasons.
I have heard that people get it tattooed
on their wrists and necks as a constant
reminder to not betray their own soul.

I thought of getting one too.

But then, honesty comes in a lot of forms other than
the breathtakingly beautiful blossoms and doesn't
usually look even half this pleasant.
In fact, I mostly see it being downright ugly.
Not to mention, insensitive, unnecessary,
and quite honestly, honesty is painful.

Honesty is people walking away.

It's broken promises because sometimes it is okay to.
It's people telling you that you hurt them and
you telling people that they hurt you.
It's people being sorry without
wanting to mend things.

It's friends whining and lovers leaving
because they don't/can't or shouldn't
love you anymore.
Or you can't/don't/shouldn't love
them anymore.
And, that is okay.
It is all fair as long as it is honest.

Fine. I will get the damn flower tattooed.

Am I A Realist Now?

I once tried to look at the
world like you do.
In its as-is form,
or rather, as it seems.

Where the mist on my tumbler
isn't longing for my sip.

Where quiet is just absence of
words and doesn't choose to tell much.

Where eye contact doesn't translate
to looking through.

Where clouds don't form hilarious shapes.

Where when the pricking grass makes you
itch, you don't think that it's asking you
to leave because you have plucked enough.

Where nobody runs in the rain.

Where nobody reads their favorite comics

with a torchlight to avoid unnecessary
parental intervention.

Where there is no place for metaphors,
dreams, and poetry.

Where things happen but in air.
Without a buildup or story.
Without any dots to trace a line on.

Geez! It was horrid.
What do you think of when
you close your eyes?
Stock Market?

KUNIKA JASHNANI

Antonyms Are Siblings

Antonyms are like brothers
and sisters from the same womb,
but the brother is ugly and
so is conveniently forgotten
in the matters of love.

We forget that extreme flow
of emotion leads to apathy.

If I try to paint a picture
using all the colors in my palette,
it will seem black.

Seeing wars around for
a long time makes you
disturbingly calm.

A free man has a strict
code of conduct,
excess light is blinding,
and too many words
make a conversation futile.

ABOUT THE AUTHOR

Poetess, illustrator and comedy writer, Kunika, is the author of Sappy Poems. She very much wanted to include her notable works in this bio, however, she doesn't have any yet which makes it seemingly impossible for her to write this bio any further. She also seems unaware of what all information is permissible here hence, she has asked to put unrequited information like she likes cake and her birthday falls in the month of April, just in case anyone would like to send her some.